Jesus is Risen!

Illustrated by Toni Goffe
Retold by LaVonne Neff

Tyndale House Publishers, Inc.
Wheaton, Illinois

© 1993 Hunt & Thorpe
Illustrations © 1993 by Toni Goffe
All rights reserved

Published in the United States by
Tyndale House Publishers, Inc.
Wheaton, Illinois
Published in Great Britain by
Hunt & Thorpe

ISBN 0-8423-1880-1
Printed in Singapore.

00 99 98 97 96 95 94 93
9 8 7 6 5 4 3 2 1

Contents

A Parade for Jesus

Matthew 21:1–11; Mark 11:1–11; Luke 19:28-38; John 12:12-19

It was Passover time, the biggest feast of the year. All God's people were going to Jerusalem to celebrate.

"Go find a colt that has never been ridden," Jesus told two of his friends. "Untie it and bring it to me."

Jesus' friends brought him the colt and helped him climb on. Jesus and the colt started down the road to Jerusalem.

People on their way to the feast saw Jesus and the colt. They remembered that he had healed their friends. They remembered that he had taught them about God. "Hosanna!" they cried out.

They threw their coats into the road to make a path for Jesus.

Children ran beside Jesus and the colt. "Hosanna!" they sang.

They threw palm branches into the road to make the path green and beautiful.

"Jesus is king!" the people shouted. "Blessings on the one who comes in the name of the Lord!"

The Last Supper

Matthew 26:17-35; Mark 14:12-31; Luke 22:7-23

Peter and John prepared the Passover supper for Jesus and ten of their friends. The thirteen men met in an upstairs room.

Jesus took some bread. He said a blessing, broke the bread, and gave it to his friends. "Eat this," he said. "This is my body. Do this in memory of me."

Then Jesus took a cup of wine. He gave thanks and passed it to his friends. "Drink this," he said. "This is my blood. It will be poured out to forgive sins."

His friends whispered to one another, "What is he talking about?"

"Some people do not want me to be king," Jesus said. "One of you will betray me to my enemies."

"Not me," said Peter.

Jesus looked sadly at Peter. "Before the rooster crows," he said, "you will say three times that you do not know me."

The Garden of Gethsemane
Matthew 26:36–46; Mark 14:32-42; Luke 22:39-46

Judas left supper early. He went to tell Jesus' enemies where to find Jesus.

Jesus and his other friends sang a hymn. Then they went to a garden called Gethsemane.

Suddenly Jesus felt sad and afraid. "Stay here," he said to his friends. He walked farther into the garden and threw himself onto the ground. "My Father!" he cried out. "Do not make me suffer and die! But I will do your will, not mine."

After a while Jesus went back to his friends. They

were fast asleep. "Could you not stay awake and pray for an hour?" Jesus asked. Then he left them and kept on praying.

A second time Jesus returned to his friends. Again they were asleep. "Why are you not praying?" Jesus asked.

The third time Jesus did not ask his friends to pray. "Get up!" he said. "My enemies have come to to arrest me."

Soldiers in the Garden
Matthew 26:47-56; Mark 14:43-52; Luke 22:47-53; John 18:1–11

Jesus' friends woke up suddenly. They saw flaming torches. They heard shouts. They saw Jesus and Judas walking toward each other.

Judas kissed Jesus. A crowd of angry men rushed at Jesus, waving swords and clubs. "Judas," Jesus said quietly, "are you betraying me with a kiss?"

Peter ran to Jesus' side. He drew his sword and struck out at the men. One man fell back, grabbing the right side of his head.

Peter's sword had cut his ear off.

"Put your sword away, Peter," Jesus said. "If I needed help, I could ask my Father, and he would send me hundreds of angels."

Then Jesus reached out and healed the man's ear.
The men took hold of Jesus and led him away.
Jesus' friends were terrified. Would they be captured
too? All eleven of them turned and ran for their lives.
Jesus was alone with his enemies.

Peter's Sin

Matthew 26:57-75; Mark 14:53–72; Luke 22:54–71, John 18:25–27

Peter followed Jesus from a safe distance. He saw him go into the high priest's palace. Peter went into the courtyard.

He heard the high priest say, "Tell us if you are the Son of God."

He heard Jesus answer, "I am who you say I am."

He heard the leaders say, "Jesus deserves to die."

A servant girl asked Peter, "Aren't you one of his followers?"

"I don't know what you're talking about," said Peter.

Someone else said, "You were with Jesus."

"I don't even know the man," said Peter.

Another person said, "You talk just like Jesus."

Peter cursed. "I do not know him!" he shouted.

Just then a rooster crowed. Peter remembered Jesus' words: "Before the rooster crows, you will say three times that you do not know me."

Peter burst into tears and ran outside.

The Trial

Matthew 27:1-32; Mark 15:1-22; Luke 23:1-32; John 18:28—19:16

The crowd shouted, "Crucify him!"

The governor, Pilate, was puzzled. "He has done nothing wrong," he said.

The crowd roared louder, "Crucify him!"

"Do you want me to crucify your king?" asked Pilate.

"Caesar is our only king," the people cried.

Pilate washed his hands. "I am innocent of this man's blood," he said. "Do whatever you like."

The soldiers beat Jesus. They spat on him and pushed a crown of thorns onto his head. They knelt before him, chanting, "Hail, King Jesus!" Then they put a heavy wooden cross on Jesus' bleeding back.

Jesus took a step and stumbled. He took another step and fell.

A soldier saw an African man, Simon of Cyrene, in the crowd. "Come and help," he ordered, placing the cross on Simon's shoulders.

The crowd moved toward Golgotha, the place of the skull.

The Crucifixion
Matthew 27:33-56; Mark 15:23-41: Luke 23:33-49; John 19:17-30

The soldiers pounded big nails through Jesus' hands. They dropped the cross into a hole in the ground.

The crowd made fun of Jesus. "He said he was God's chosen one," they said. "Let's see him save himself!"

Two thieves hung on crosses next to Jesus. One

thief said to him, "Remember me when you come into your kingdom."

"I promise you," Jesus said, "that today you will be with me in paradise."

Mary, Jesus' mother, stood near the cross with Jesus' friend John. Jesus said to Mary, "John is now your son." He said to John, "Mary is now your mother."

The sky turned black. For three hours there was no light. "God," Jesus cried out, "why have you deserted me?"

Suddenly the earth began to rumble and shake. "It is finished," Jesus said. "Father, into your hands I commit my spirit."

And he bowed his head and died.

He Is Risen!
Matthew 27:57–28:8; Mark 15:42–16:8; Luke 23:50–24:8

Friday afternoon a rich man, Joseph of Arimathaea, took Jesus' body, wrapped it in a clean cloth, and put it in his own new tomb. He rolled a heavy stone across the doorway.

Saturday morning Jesus' enemies said to Pilate, "We are afraid Jesus' friends will steal his body."

Pilate sent soldiers to guard the tomb. Jesus'

enemies sealed the tomb so nobody could move the stone.

Early Sunday morning some women went to the tomb. They planned to put spices and perfumes on Jesus' body.

Pilate's soldiers were not guarding the tomb. The heavy stone was not blocking the doorway. The women tiptoed inside.

The tomb was empty!

Suddenly the women saw a man in shining clothes. "Why are you looking in a tomb for a living person?" the man asked. "Jesus is not here. He is risen! Go quickly and tell his friends the good news!"

Seeing and Believing

Luke 24:9-12, 36-49; John 20:19-21

The women ran to tell Jesus' friends. "Jesus is alive!" the women said.

The men did not believe them. Peter and John ran to the tomb to see for themselves. It was just as the women had said. The tomb was empty.

What could this mean? Had Jesus' body been stolen? Would they be blamed? Jesus' friends were frightened. They hid in a room and locked the door.

Suddenly Jesus was in the room. "Peace be with you," he said.

The door was still locked. Were they seeing a ghost? "Touch me," said Jesus. "A ghost does not have flesh and bones."

The men timidly reached out and touched Jesus. He was warm. He felt real.

"Is there anything here to eat?" asked Jesus. The men gave him a piece of grilled fish. Jesus ate it hungrily.

The men looked at each other and smiled. "He is risen!" they shouted.

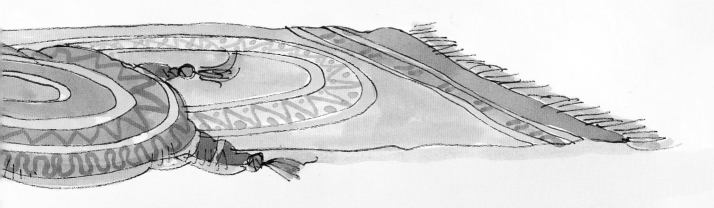

Jesus Forgives Peter

John 21:1-19

Peter, John, and five other men had fished all night. They had caught nothing.

At daybreak they saw a man standing on the shore. He called out, "Throw the net on the right side of the boat." They did, and fish swarmed in.

"It's Jesus!" John said. The men turned toward shore, where Jesus was cooking fish over a charcoal fire.

After breakfast Jesus turned to Peter. "Peter, do you love me?" he asked.

"Yes, you know I love you," said Peter.

"Peter, do you love me?" Jesus asked again.

"Yes, you know I love you," said Peter.

"Peter, do you love me?" Jesus asked a third time.

"You know everything," said Peter. "You know I love you."

Jesus smiled, and suddenly Peter understood. Three times Peter had said he did not know Jesus. Now Jesus was forgiving him.

"Follow me," said Jesus. And Peter did.